Becoming

ISBN 0-8378-2046-4
GB683

Becoming

·Hazelden Encouragements·

Illustrated by
Jody Bishel and Daniel Buckley

The C.R. Gibson Company
Norwalk, Connecticut 06856

The Journey

The great thing in this world
is not so much where we are,
but in what direction
we are moving.

Oliver Wendell Holmes

Growth and change take us along an ever-changing road. Sometimes the way is hard and craggy. Sometimes we climb mountains. Sometimes we slide down the other side on a toboggan.

Sometimes we rest.

Sometimes we grope through the darkness. Sometimes we're blinded by sunlight.

At times many may walk with us on the road; sometimes we feel nearly alone.

Ever changing, always interesting, always leading someplace better, someplace good.

What a journey!

Melody Beattie

Our most effective use of each day means believing we can accomplish something. There is time to be grateful for each day's experiences. There is time to build relationships with ourselves and others. Each day there is time to grow.

Life is a series of opportunities
for emotional, spiritual and intellectual growth.
No opportunity for action is beyond our capabilities.

I am becoming.
And with becoming,
comes peace.

We are becoming,
every moment of time.
Discovering who
and what we really are,
alone and with one another,
is worthy of celebration.

Change surrounds us. It lies within us, too. The trees in the yard have changed. They've grown taller. Their leaves die and scatter on the ground in the fall. We don't resemble our baby pictures much more, either. Like trees, we've grown up.

Some changes we don't notice while they're going on. The snow melts; the birds fly south; our hair grows a little every day. Other changes startle us. A best friend moves away. Perhaps a favorite grandparent dies.

We have to remember that change is as natural as breathing. We can't keep it from happening, but we can trust that change never means to harm us. It's a sign of growing up.

Life is a process.
It is never static,
always moving; always inviting us
to participate fully.

Focusing our attention outside of ourselves on hobbies, on goals, on friends, steadily bathes us with inspiration and enthusiasm for moving forward. It is true that happiness lies within us; but our discovery of this is only made possible by our willing involvement in the lives and experiences surrounding us.

Liking ourselves doesn't mean
we approve of certain traits or behaviors.
But we can accept them.
We aren't the most perfect companion,
lover, friend or parent.
Neither is anyone else.

*It is only by forgetting yourself
that you draw near to God.*

Henry David Thoreau

There is magic in the realization that our acquaintances, our co-workers and neighbors, are presented to us by design. When we step away from the circle of people calling to us, we are denying them the opportunities for growth they may need and preventing it in ourselves as well. We need one another and being helped by someone else fulfills more needs than our own.

*Succeeding alone
means we have survived;
succeeding with others
means we have truly lived.*

The Ebb and Flow

I accept life unconditionally...
Most people ask for happiness on condition.
Happiness can only be felt
if you don't set any condition.

Arthur Rubenstein

Life is flowing and continuous; it is full of crossroads, tributaries, and sudden bends. To live is to travel, and navigable space attracts us. We want to follow the road or the river to find what lies around the next bend, over the next rise.

No one has ever lived our lives before us. Many past events have prepared us for this moment, and we may feel as though we were following a track that has been laid out for us. But at other times we feel as though we were strapped to the nose of a rocket, plunging through space where no one has ever been.

Everything in nature changes. We can trust the sun and moon will rise and set, the tide will ebb and flow, and the seasons will change. Because we can trust these things to happen, we can learn to trust the fact that extremes in nature are normal.

The grand essentials
to happiness in life
are something to do,
something to love
and something to hope for.

Joseph Addison

*O*ur lives are patchwork quilts of mismatched fabrics. The tattered scraps of quarrels, the brilliant colors of our happy moments, even our cold, white doubts and emptiness—all these are stitched together by an invisible seamstress.

The green thread of growth holds the colors together. Often we want to cut away a square of painful memory. But without it, our quilt would lose its beauty, for contrast would disappear. If a piece is removed, the whole is weakened and incomplete.

*O*ur freedom to make mistakes is one of our greatest assets, for this is the way we learn humility, persistence, courage to take risks, and better ways of doing things. Since mistakes are natural aspects of growth, we can salute them in ourselves and others as signs of life.

*I shall enjoy the richness of today.
My life is weaving an intricate,
necessary pattern
that is uniquely mine.*

*I will be grateful
for the experiences today
that give my tapestry its beauty.*

Rainy Days

As rain restores the earth,
rest restores the spirit.

Anonymous

ainy days slow us down. We are busy
people, driving ourselves to go places
and get things done. But rain seems to slow life
down.

Slowing down can show us the peace in our
lives, the peace of knowing we have all we need
right inside us. The pressures of the world can
drop away for a time while we reflect.

As the rain soaks into the ground, its serenity
enters our hearts. Leaves on trees look more
green. Plants and flowers are no longer thirsty.
When we slow down, we can be comforted by
what we have in our hearts, knowing everything
is going to be all right.

We can plan a small gift for ourselves—a walk by the lake, for instance. In our excitement with a rush of events, we often forget that we, like the infants we once were, need to take a rest and reenergize.

When we are tired,
we are attacked by ideas
we conquered long ago.

Friedrich Wilhelm Nietzsche

Many times our late night thinking
is like a late movie,
scary, poor quality
and makes little sense.

here isn't a day that won't have some lightness. There isn't a night that won't have a rising sun at its end. There isn't a problem that won't have a solution; a teardrop that won't have a smile; a weary soul that won't be energized once again. Tonight we can sing, for we have faith in the rising sun.

Today I will do something special for me.

Good Days

*Keep your face in the sunshine
and you cannot see the shadow.*

Helen Keller

Let's make a calendar of wonderful anniversaries: This is the day I first heard tender words from someone dear; this is the day I stopped smoking; ten years ago on this day I committed myself to a program of positive living and spiritual growth.

Keeping such a calendar, even for a short time, gives us a record of spiritual progress. To be able to say, "How different I am from what I was five years ago" can be a truly cheering thing.

Life can only be understood backwards,
but it must be lived forwards.

Soren Kierkegaard

*T*here is a saying, "a ship in the harbor is safe." But ships weren't made to stay in harbors. We captain our own ships and when we sail, we are taking risks. There will be calm sailing, but there will also be ferocious storms. We will weather anything with a supportive crew and a determined belief to guide us.

*H*ope is the only bee
that makes honey
without flowers.

Robert Ingersoll

I t's up to us to recognize our victories. We can celebrate such joyous times with a smile or a nod, a notation in a journal, or by sharing it with a special person in our lives. Victory after victory, we will come to realize the most important thing about our achievements is not outside recognition, but the peaceful, satisfied feeling we have inside.

A boy once asked his grandfather how he had become so happy and successful in his life. "Right decisions," replied his grandfather. The boy thought for a while and then asked a second question. "But how do you learn to make right decisions?" The grandfather answered quickly with a twinkle in his eye, "Wrong decisions!"

*T*ime brings summer to a close as well as winter to an end. Time ages the brilliant petals of flowers as well as prepares the new buds. Time brings the end to a life as well as the beginning to another. Because of this continuum, we can trust that time will bring the good to us as well as take away the bad.

Every day is a training ground, and every experience trains me to recognize the value of succeeding experiences. With richness, I am developing, one moment at a time.

∼

You have the opportunity to think creatively and rely on your inner guide. Instead of dreading the unfamiliar, be glad for it. It's moving you closer to understanding life's mysteries.

Not Alone

When you have shut the doors,
and darkened your room,
remember never to say
that you are alone;
for God is within
and your genius is within,
and what need have they of light
to see what you are doing?

Epictetus

*N*one of us is ever alone, especially at night. The methods we use to fall asleep peacefully are good, but we need to remember there are always three angels that guard our sleep.

The first angel is our Higher Power, the second is the positive side of our minds that believes in us. The third is our gentle, hopeful spirit within. Whether we know they are there during the day isn't as important as knowing they are there at night. We are at peace in our sleep because they are there to watch over us.

When I don't feel close to God, who moved?

So often we think we're alone, but we never are. We each have a Higher Power just waiting to be relied on. Nothing is too difficult or fearful for us to handle with the help of our Higher Power. When we develop the habit of letting our Higher Power ease our way, our fears are gone.

I am satisfied that,
when the Almighty wants me to do
or not to do a particular thing,
[God] finds a way of letting me know.

Abraham Lincoln

God is real. Loving. Good. Caring. God wants to give us all the good we can handle. The more we turn our mind and heart toward a positive understanding of God, the more God validates us. The more we thank God for who God is, who we are, and the exact nature of our present circumstance, the more God acts in our behalf.

In fact, all along, God planned to act in our behalf. God is Creator, Benefactor, and Source. God has shown me, beyond all else, that how I come to understand God is not nearly as important as knowing God understands me.

Melody Beattie

*Faith is the bird
that feels the light
when the dawn is still dark.*

Rabindranath Tagore

In the darkness of early morning the bird outside the window begins to sing. Soon the eastern sky turns pink. The bird continues singing until the first yellow rays warm its soft wings. Then it flies away, not returning to the window until the next morning.

We can learn from the small bird. We can start by singing a song to celebrate the new day—a day that we have faith will warm our hearts and shed light on our actions. Like the bird's faith in the sunrise, we need only to have faith that God meant each day to enrich our lives.

When we seek God's will and direction, we open the door to a Power greater than our own. We place our burdens on Someone's shoulders who can bear the weight. We admit that we are not strong enough to carry the tremendous load we thought it was our responsibility to bear. And we surrender to the fact that we do not have sufficient knowledge or understanding to resolve our quandaries alone.

*Love is a great thing,
a good above all others,
which alone maketh every burden light.
Love is watchful,
and whilst sleeping still keeps watch;
though fatigued, it is not weary;
though pressed, it is not forced.*

Thomas Kempis

*I am moving and changing
and growing at the right pace.
What is right for me
will come to me.
I will let the joy
of becoming warm me.*

Colophon

Compiled and edited by Stephanie C. Oda
Designed by Aurora Campanella Lyman
Calligraphed by Martin Holloway
Type set in Kunstler Script, Bodoni Book Italic